LADYBIRD  HIS

ROMANS

91120000193152

History consultant: Philip Parker
Map illustrator: Martin Sanders

A catalogue record for this book is available from the British Library

Published by Ladybird Books Ltd
80 Strand, London, WC2R 0RL
A Penguin Company

001

© LADYBIRD BOOKS LTD MMXIV

LADYBIRD and the device of a Ladybird are trademarks of Ladybird Books Ltd.

All rights reserved. No part of this publication may be reproduced,
stored in a retrieval system, or transmitted in any form or by any means,
electronic, mechanical, photocopying, recording or otherwise,
without the prior consent of the copyright owner.

ISBN: 978-0-72327-730-9
Printed in China

LADYBIRD HISTORIES

ROMANS

Written by Simon Adams
Main illustrations by Emmanuel Cerisier
Cartoon illustrations by Clive Goodyer

Contents

BRENT LIBRARIES	
KIL	
91120000193152	
Askews & Holts	04-Jul-2014
J937.06 JUNIOR NON-F	£7.99

Who Were the Romans?

The vast Roman Empire existed between 3,000 and 1,500 years ago. It has now completely disappeared, yet we are still fascinated by the Romans. We study their history and culture. We visit the remains of their cities and buildings. We watch films about their heroes, and read books that describe their lives. So who were the Romans? And why should we care about them today?

The Romans began as a small tribe living in central Italy in the 700s BCE. They built a village on the hills by the River Tiber that eventually became the city of Rome. From these beginnings they went on to create an empire that stretched across most of Europe, North Africa and the Middle East. This vast empire eventually collapsed during the 400s CE.

Roman legacies

Much of our modern world is the result of what the Romans created. Our languages, government, laws, churches, calendars, and names of our months and planets all have Roman origins. The skills of Roman builders and engineers were such that many buildings, aqueducts and roads around the world are well-preserved and even still in use today.

Daily life in ancient Rome

The Founding of Rome

According to an ancient story, Rome was originally founded by two brothers. We don't know if this is entirely true, but archaeological remains seem to suggest that a city was built around the same time as the events in the story.

Romulus and Remus

The story says that twins called Romulus and Remus were born into a royal family in central Italy. Their great-uncle, Amulius, wanted to be king in their place, so he ordered his soldiers to throw the twins into the River Tiber. Luckily, Romulus and Remus were found by a she-wolf and a shepherd then gave them a home. When the brothers grew up, they killed Amulius and around 753 CE began to plan a new city. But the twins soon argued about where to build it. In the end, Romulus killed Remus and named the city 'Rome' after himself.

Early Rome

The founding of Rome is more likely to have happened like this. Around 800 BCE, a small Italian tribe began to build villages of huts and other buildings on hills by the River Tiber. These villages slowly grew to form a single city that eventually spread over seven hills. Romulus became the first king of this new city.

The Roman writer Livy said in his history of Rome that the city was founded in the perfect place: in the centre of Italy in a high position, near a river that could be used for trade to and from the Mediterranean coast. This was only partly true. The River Tiber often flooded; and the land was mostly marsh.

The Roman Republic

After the death of Romulus in 717 BCE, a series of kings ruled Rome. One, Tarquinius Priscus, came to power in 616 BCE. He made many vital improvements to the city, draining the marshes and building a public square. New, strong buildings were built of stone.

The seventh king, Tarquinius Superbus – whose name means 'Tarquin the Proud' – was very unpopular. In 509 BCE the Romans rebelled and threw Tarquinius out of the city. In his place they set up a republic, in which Rome would be ruled by its people.

Governing Rome

Three hundred of Rome's most powerful men formed the Senate, which passed laws for the new Republic. These men mostly came from the patricians, the class of richest citizens. They gave day-to-day control of the city to two consuls. The common people, known as plebeians, had little power, while women and slaves had none. In 494 BCE the unhappy plebeians elected their own representatives, or tribunes, to look after their interests. Eventually, plebeians won the right to become consuls, too.

Members of the Roman Senate

10

Enemies of Rome

Rome had many enemies. First the Romans defeated the neighbouring Latin, Volscian and Sabine tribes, and then they captured the powerful cities of the Etruscans. Their biggest threat, though, came from the Gauls of France, who had by then settled in northern Italy. In 390 BCE the Gauls attacked Rome and burned most of it to the ground. The Romans rebuilt their city and surrounded it with a 10-kilometre-long wall. After further wars against the Samnites and Greeks, the Romans eventually took control of central and southern Italy.

A Gaul soldier

Saved by the geese

One night the Gauls tried to quietly enter Rome. They disturbed some local geese, which made such a noise that the Roman soldiers woke up and were able to fight off the intruders.

Fighting Carthage

The most powerful force in the Mediterranean Sea was the trading city of Carthage in North Africa. Over the course of three long wars, Rome fought Carthage for control of the sea. By the end of the last war, Carthage was no more and Rome held territories in Sicily, Spain, Sardinia and North Africa.

The First Punic War

The first war broke out in 264 BCE over control of the southern Italian island of Sicily. The Carthaginians had a big navy but the Romans had none. So they copied an old Carthaginian ship and built a large navy of their own. At first, the Romans were unsuccessful, but in 241 BCE they gained a massive naval victory and won the war. Sicily was theirs.

The deadly spike

During the first Punic War, the Romans developed the corvus, a plank with a spike on the end that they carried on their ships. When they got close to the enemy, they dropped the corvus on to the enemy ship so that it gripped the deck. Soldiers then poured over the corvus into the ship and fought the enemy to the death.

The second and third wars

The second Punic war broke out in 218 BCE. The Carthaginian general Hannibal marched his army and thirty-seven war elephants from Spain, through France and over the Alps into Italy, catching the Romans by surprise. Hannibal won many famous victories against the Romans but eventually he was defeated outside Carthage in 202 BCE. Carthage now held only a small part of North Africa but the Romans still feared it.

In 149 BCE Rome went to war for a third time. Roman armies besieged Carthage and finally broke into the city in 146 BCE. The 50,000 surviving Carthaginians became slaves and their city was destroyed forever.

Hannibal's huge army consisted of soldiers, cavalry, horses, elephants and baggage animals. It took the army fifteen days of marching in harsh weather conditions to reach Italy.

The Roman Army

The power behind the expansion of Rome was its great army. Roman soldiers were well armed and equipped, highly trained and very disciplined. Many people consider the Roman army to be the greatest fighting force of all time.

A Roman legion

The army was made up of infantry units known as legions, each with over 5,000 men. As well as 4,800 soldiers, legions also included a doctor, cooks, engineers, builders, horseback messengers and others. One legion broke down as:

Eight men = one contubernium (8 men)
Ten contubernia = one century (80 men + one centurion)
Six centuries = one cohort (480 men)
Ten cohorts = one legion (4,800 men)

A centurion and his century. You might expect a Roman military century to contain 100 men, just as a century of time contains 100 years. In fact, it contained only eighty men.

Auxiliaries

Only full Roman citizens could become legionaries, while other people ruled by the Romans could become auxiliaries. Some of these auxiliaries, such as the highly skilled Syrian archers, formed their own military units. Auxiliaries served for longer in the army than legionaries (twenty-five years) and were paid less. Once they finished their service, however, they earned the right to became full Roman citizens.

The Tortoise

To protect themselves in battle from arrows and other missiles, the Roman soldiers used to advance with their shields over their heads and round their sides. With this wall of shields round them, they looked rather like a tortoise's shell!

Roman Roads

Many people think that all Roman roads were completely straight, and that all roads led to Rome. Both facts are *almost* true.

Planning the road

The Romans built their roads as flat and straight as possible so that the legionaries could march quickly from one military base to another. Merchants also used the roads, as did farmers and traders.

Roman engineers first planned a new road by placing a series of marker points on the ground. These probably consisted of sticks, or bonfires in wooded areas. When the markers were joined together to form the route, they created a series of straight lines linked together with only minor curves.

Building the road

Then the ground was dug up. Large stones were laid down and then covered by layers of smaller stones and gravel. Paving stones were sometimes laid on top. The finished road was usually around 1 metre thick and up to 9 metres wide. It sloped down at the sides to allow water to drain away.

Roads connected major Roman towns and cities together, as well as military bases. Most importantly, all these roads connected in to other roads that led to Rome.

Miles and miles

A Roman mile was 1.48 kilometres long. Milestones along the roads gave the distance to Rome or nearby towns, and many also had the name of the current emperor carved on them.

The Romans built around 80,000 kilometres of roads, with up to 10,000 kilometres in Britain alone. The labour was usually done by slaves.

17

Julius Caesar

One of the most famous Roman leaders was Julius Caesar. He was born in 100 BCE and became a military commander. Caesar's armies conquered Gaul (France) and twice crossed the English Channel to attack Britain.

Crossing the Rubicon

After the end of the Punic wars with Carthage, Roman generals held great political power and often fought amongst themselves for control of Rome.

One such leader, Pompey the Great, allied himself with Caesar, but the two soon fell out. In 49 BCE, Pompey and the Senate ordered Caesar home from Gaul without his army. When he got to the River Rubicon in northern Italy, Caesar paused. The river marked the boundary between Gaul and Italy. If he crossed the river with his army against Rome's wishes that meant he had declared civil war. Caesar made his decision and moved his army across the river. Once in Rome, he seized control and was made dictator.

Dictator of Rome

Caesar was a great leader. He reorganized the government and reformed the tax system. He also tried to help the poor. Most importantly, he introduced the 365 and one-quarter day Julian calendar we still use today. In February 44 BCE the Senate made him dictator for life, which meant he had absolute power. A month later, though, on 15 March (known as the Ides of March) he was stabbed to death by enemies in the Senate.

Julius Caesar crossing the Rubicon

Creating the Empire

Julius Caesar's death began a period of civil war that lasted until 30 BCE. Three years after the war, the Roman Republic came to an end and Rome became an Empire.

Civil war

After Caesar's death his great-nephew Octavian learned that Caesar had adopted him as his son and heir. Octavian wanted revenge on those who had killed Caesar, but Mark Antony, a Roman politican and general, was supporting an uneasy peace. The two eventually joined up to defeat the killers in 42 BCE in northern Greece. They then shared power, with Octavian taking the western half of the republic and Mark Antony the eastern half. Tensions continued though, and in 32 BCE Octavian was strong enough to fight Mark Antony. His fleet, led by the commander Agrippa, defeated Mark Antony and the Egyptians at Actium, on the western coast of Greece, in 31 BCE.

The first emperor

Octavian was now the unchallenged ruler of Rome. He offered to return his power to the Senate but this was refused. In 27 BCE the Senate gave him a new name. They called him Augustus, meaning the 'deeply respected one' and gave him a new title, *imperator,* or 'supreme commander'. In this way, Augustus became the first emperor of Rome.

Cleopatra

Mark Antony fell in love with the Egyptian queen Cleopatra, but this relationship made the Romans uneasy. The following year, after the Romans had defeated the Egyptians at Actium, both Mark Antony and Cleopatra took their lives.

The Battle of Actium was fought at sea, on big warships known as 'galleys'.

The Roman Empire

Augustus was the first in a long line of emperors that ruled until 476 CE. During that time, the Roman Empire grew until it reached its greatest extent in the year 117 CE, under the emperor Trajan. By then it stretched 4,000 kilometres east from the Atlantic Ocean to the Persian Gulf and was home to more than 50 million people.

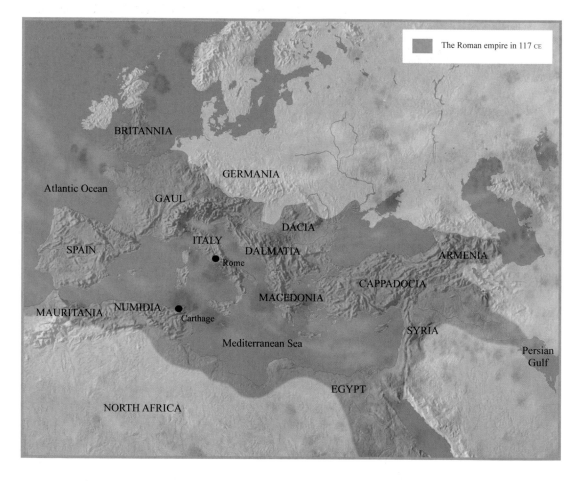

The Roman empire in 117 CE

The succession of one emperor after another did not always run smoothly. Four emperors struggled for power in the year 69 CE. Five emperors fought for control in 193 CE, and for much of the 200s warring rivals fought each other.

Divide and rule

The Empire had become too big for one man to rule, so in 285 CE Diocletian appointed another emperor to rule alongside him. Years later, the emperor Constantine moved the Empire's capital from Rome to the new city of Constantinople, now Istanbul in Turkey. Finally, in 395 CE the Empire was split into separate western and eastern halves, each with its own capital. This made the Empire easier to run.

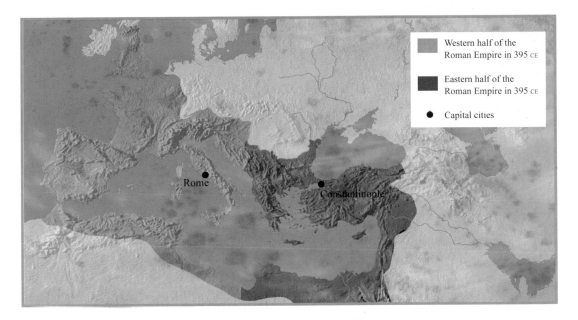

Western half of the Roman Empire in 395 CE

Eastern half of the Roman Empire in 395 CE

● Capital cities

Rome

Constantinople

Constantinople literally translates as 'Constantine's City'.

Conquering Britain

The Romans made three attempts to conquer Britain. The last and successful invasion in 43 CE ended up leading to almost 400 years of Roman rule.

The first Roman invasion occurred in 55 BCE. It was a punishment for some British tribes helping the Gauls resist Julius Caesar's attempt at conquering Gaul. The invasion was unsuccessful, so Caesar returned the following year with a large invasion force. He defeated a British force north of the River Thames and returned to Gaul. Britain was then left in peace for a century, until Claudius became emperor in 41 CE.

Claudius wanted a military victory to establish his power, so he sent a large force to conquer Britain. The Romans landed in Kent and marched to London and on to Colchester, where they defeated the powerful Catuvellaunian kingdom. From then on, they steadily expanded their power until they controlled the whole of England and Wales.

Roman rule in Britain

The Romans established the capital of the province of Britannia (as they called Britain) in Londinium (London). They also built many other towns and cities, notably Verulamium (St Albans) and Eboracum (York). They connected these cities with long straight roads and supplied them with running water and hot baths. Military forts also housed troops to prevent rebellions or invasions by foreign barbarians.

London Wall

The Romans surrounded London with a protective wall. The wall was 6 metres high and 2.5 metres thick and stretched for 5 kilometres. The Roman wall stood for 1,600 years and still roughly forms the boundary of the modern-day City of London.

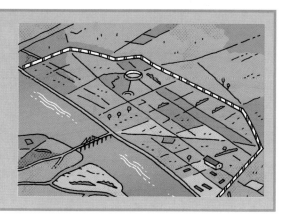

Caesar's troops landed on the Kent coast.

Fortifications

In 117 CE Hadrian became Emperor of Rome. The Empire had been growing for years and Hadrian decided it had got big enough. He instead wanted to make it stronger within its existing borders, and ordered fortifications to be built where those borders were dangerous and vulnerable to attack.

Hadrian's Wall

In the north of England Roman Britain faced war-like tribes, such as the Picts and Caledonians. To protect Britain Hadrian built a long wall all the way across the country from the Irish Sea to just short of the North Sea to mark the border and keep enemies out. Most of the wall is still visible today. It is 117 kilometres long, 3 metres wide and up to 4 metres high, and is mainly built of stone with smaller sections of turf.

In Roman times castles, turrets and watchtowers were placed along the length of the wall, housing soldiers on the lookout for enemy action.

The Roman *limites*

The weakest stretch of border in the Roman Empire was in Germany, so Hadrian built a massive wooden wall on the border between the Rhine and Danube rivers. It consisted of a 450-kilometre-long fence containing many watchtowers. Soldiers were housed in barracks along its length. The land in front of the fence was filled with ditches, moats, sharpened stakes with metal points, and other devices to keep enemies out.

Letters home

Soldiers stationed on Hadrian's Wall were often cold and homesick for the warm lands they had left behind. The Vindolanda tablets are surviving examples of letters that were sent home by soldiers, which were written on thin pieces of wood-bark.

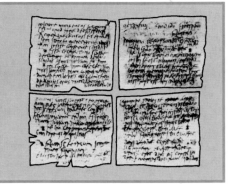

Imperial Rome

By the time Augustus became the first emperor in 27 BCE Rome was one of the largest cities in the world. More than 1 million people lived there. But Rome was not a grand city. It had muddy streets, shabby houses and dull public buildings. The river often flooded. Augustus decided to rebuild the city as the grandest capital of the Empire.

Augustus set up a police service to keep order and a fire service to put out fires. He had the river dredged to prevent flooding and built a new bridge across it. He constructed new public baths and improved the water supply to the city. He got rid of many narrow streets. Above all, he built many fine public buildings, including law courts, temples and theatres.

Roman citizens enjoyed sharing the splendid public buildings, even though many still lived in poor conditions.

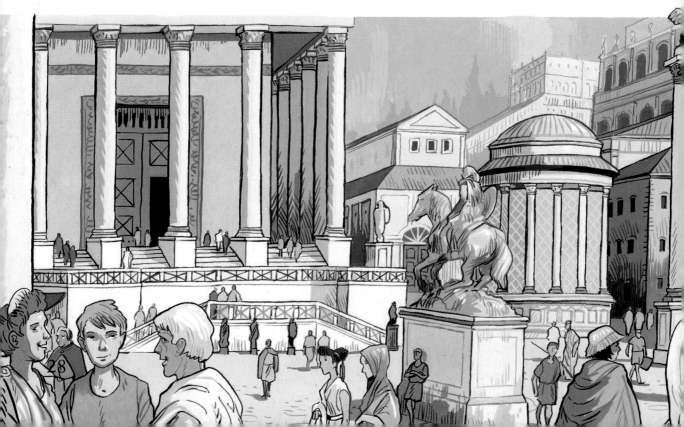

Shining stone

One impressive thing Augustus did was to improve the look of the city. Many important Roman buildings were made of red brick, but he covered them with white and coloured marble so that they shone in the sun. He boasted that he had found a city built of brick and left it in marble.

The Horologium of Augustus

In the centre of Rome, Augustus erected a vast obelisk called the Horologium. This was designed to show the length of shadows cast by the sun at midday, a way of telling what day of the year it was.

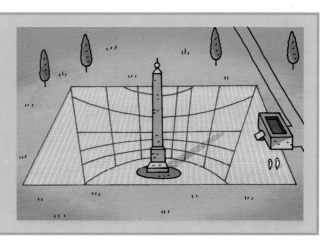

The Colosseum

Most Roman towns and cities had their own amphitheatres. These were huge open-air arenas used to stage fights in front of an audience. Here, gladiators fought each other, sometimes to the death, for the entertainment of the crowd.

The largest amphitheatre in the Roman Empire was in Rome. It was called the Colosseum and opened in 80 CE. The Colosseum staged a full day of entertainment around 100 times a year. Each day started with a parade of gladiators, musicians, jugglers and other entertainers. Then came the wild animals, including lions, bears or even crocodiles. Armed hunters fought these beasts. Criminals were then thrown into the ring to be torn to pieces and killed by the animals.

Gladiators

The gladiator fights were the highlight of the day's events. Different types of gladiator fought each other with swords, nets and other weapons. If a gladiator was injured he could ask the referee – or the emperor if he was present – to stop the fight. After the crowd had cheered or booed, the emperor would make his final decision. If he gestured with his thumbs down, a gladiator was to be spared. Most gladiators were spared, as it was expensive to train them.

At the end of their fighting lives gladiators were given a wooden sword, which was a sign that they did not have to fight any more and were now free.

Sea battles

The Colosseum was sometimes flooded with water so that pretend naval battles could be held between small warships.

Most gladiators were prisoners-of-war, criminals or slaves, though some were volunteers.

A Day at the Races

The Romans loved all sport, but they especially loved chariot racing. Most cities had special oval tracks where chariots raced for prizes. The chariot racetrack in Rome was called the Circus Maximus.

The Circus Maximus was vast. It was approximately 620 metres long, 150 metres wide and could fit in 250,000 spectators. This is bigger than any modern-day sports stadium. Spectators turned up early for the best seats. They bought food and drink from stalls by the track and placed bets on who would win.

Most racing chariots were pulled by teams of two or four horses, but teams of six or eight horses were also sometimes used.

At speed

The chariots raced in teams. The four teams in Rome were the Reds, Whites, Blues and Greens, all owned by the emperor. Up to twelve chariots competed in each race. The race consisted of seven laps of the Circus Maximus, around 8 kilometres.

Charioteers were mostly slaves, although some were highly paid professionals. Chariot racing was fast and dangerous, especially round the tight corners, where many crashes happened. The winning chariot driver received a palm leaf, a gold necklace and some money.

Other entertainment

Many Romans also enjoyed the theatre. Plays included comedies, tragedies and mimes. Successful actors were treated like modern film stars. Women were not allowed in the front rows of the theatre in case they ran off with a good-looking actor!

Life in the City

The idea we have today of ancient Rome is that it was full of great buildings and large ceremonial arches. Some wealthy Romans did live in huge houses with luxuries like running water and fine furnishings, but most ordinary Romans lived in cramped, overcrowded apartment blocks called *insulae*.

Home life

Most houses in Rome were blocks of three or four storeys. The ground floor contained shops and workshops that people could walk into from the street. Above them were two or three floors of small flats or single rooms. The water supply did not reach above the first floor. Everyone shared the same toilet. Most blocks had no heating systems. People burned logs for cooking, hot water and to keep warm in winter. Not surprisingly, house fires were very common.

Street life

The streets of Rome were busy during the day. Shopkeepers displayed their goods for sale and citizens were out and about on their daily business. The main roads were swept clean, but smaller roads were left dirty. Many people threw their rubbish out into the street. At night, there were no streetlights, so it was completely dark. It was unsafe to walk the unlit streets, as thieves lay in wait.

The Romans did not have the supermarkets or large department stores we have today. Instead, each shop specialized in just one type of produce.

Keeping watch

Emperor Augustus set up teams of vigiles, slaves who acted as firefighters and night watchmen. Their nickname was spartoli, or 'little bucket fellows' as they put out fires with buckets of water.

Wonderful Water

One of the Romans' greatest achievements was creating a constant supply of fresh running water for everyday use, such as drinking, cooking, washing, bathing and for public fountains. This fresh water supply was well ahead of its time. Most European towns did not have a similar service until the 1800s, over 1,000 years later!

Running water

In order to get fresh water many towns were built near rivers or springs. Others were supplied with water brought in by aqueducts. These were gently sloping pipes along which water flowed from its source to large storage reservoirs. Lead pipes then carried the water to fountains, from where people collected the water they needed. Some rich households had their own water supply piped into their houses. They also had a system to collect rainwater from the roof.

Toilet time

The Romans built communal lavatories without any doors. Up to twelve people could use these lavatories at any one time. They sat on a row or semicircle of stone seats. Some had wooden seats for more comfort. Dirty water from the public baths flowed under the seats to wash the waste away.

Roman baths

Every Roman town also had its own public baths. These included hot and cold pools, steam rooms and saunas, with separate areas for men and women. Slaves massaged oil into people's skin, then scraped it off with a strigil, which also removed dirt and dead skin.

Some Roman baths were filled from natural hot springs, but in others underground furnaces provided hot water for the baths. They also pumped hot air under the floor and behind the walls to heat the saunas.

People came to the baths to wash and relax, but the baths were often used as public meeting places, too.

Life in the Country

Many Romans lived in small villages in the countryside. They farmed the land, producing food, drink, wool and other products. Rich Romans from the cities also built large luxury villas in the country, where they could relax.

Crops

The Romans grew similar crops to the ones we grow today. Grapevines and olives grew in the warmer south, with grain grown throughout the Empire. Common fruits included grapes, peaches, pears, plums and apples, as well as many different nuts. Herbs were grown for both cooking and medicine.

Farms

The first Roman farms were small, producing just enough food for the owners to feed themselves. During the wars with Carthage from 264 to 146 BCE, many farmers left their land as Roman territories expanded in Italy, Spain and North Africa. Rich landowners then bought up the farms and created vast country estates known as *latifundia*. Just six men were said to have owned half the Roman province of Africa!

These new farms produced lots of food, as well as earning a lot of money for their owners. Slaves were the main labourers and were forced to work long hours.

Landowners often hired men to oversee the day-to-day running of their farms.

The Roman Family

The family was the centre of Roman life. The *paterfamilias*, or father, was the head of the household. He had authority over everyone in the house.

For work, aristocratic men took part in public and political life. Others fought in the army or worked for the government. Lower-class Roman men held jobs such as merchant, porter, weaponsmith or builder.

Women

Roman women usually married in their early teens. They were then in charge of looking after the home and the children. They also controlled the money used to buy shopping and pay bills. Women could inherit, own and sell property. Otherwise, they had few legal rights and were excluded from public life, apart from the very few who became priestesses.

Working women

There were not many jobs for women. Some were hairdressers, worked in a shop, or helped to deliver new babies. Weaving and making clothes was usually a wife's job.

Slaves in the household

Rich Romans owned slaves to work in their houses, businesses and farms. Slaves were considered the property of their owners. These slaves were mainly prisoners-of-war, but some were the children of slaves already working in the home. Slaves were bought and sold in the local market by slave dealers. A few educated slaves could became teachers or doctors and earn money. Only their master could free them, although they could save up to buy their freedom if they wanted.

A large, rich household could have over 100 slaves.

Roman Children

Roman children were brought up to serve the Roman Empire. They had to respect their fathers and maintain the good name of their families.

 Children were named when they were eight or nine days old. They were then given a lucky charm, called a *bulla*, to keep evil spirits away.

Children usually had two first names and a surname. Boys were often named after their fathers. A girl's name was sometimes a female version of her father's name: Fabia Honorata, for example, was the daughter of Fabius Honoratus.

Toys

Children had many different toys that reflected the world around them. Babies played with pottery rattles shaped like birds, with stones inside to make a noise. Older children had toy animals, hobby horses, see-saws, swings, marbles and hoops to roll along the ground. Younger children played with dolls made of wood, clay or linen stuffed with rags or fought with pretend wooden spears.

Carved wooden toy

Bird-shaped rattle

Simple linen doll

Education

The only children who went to school were those from wealthy families. The children of the very rich were educated at home by private teachers, while the children of the poor had no education at all.

Boys, and some girls, learned reading, writing and arithmetic from the ages of seven to eleven at the local *ludus* (primary school). A few boys then went on to the *grammaticus* (secondary school), where they studied Greek and Roman literature, history, astronomy, mathematics, geography, music and athletics. This prepared them for a life in the army or government. Girls did not study for any career as they were expected to marry. Instead, they stayed at home to learn home-making skills.

Roman children wrote lessons on a wax tablet. They used an iron, bronze or bone stylus, a type of pen, to scratch the letters into the wax. When they had finished they rubbed out the letters so that they could start again the next day.

43

Food and Lifestyle

The Romans didn't have many of the foods we enjoy today, such as tomatoes, potatoes or chocolate, but they loved to eat and drink and meals often became social occasions.

Poor Romans ate basic foods, such as porridge, bread and vegetable stews. Richer Romans enjoyed a more varied diet. For breakfast, they might have wheat biscuits with honey. At lunchtime they might have eaten a simple meal of cold meat, cheese, eggs and fruit. The main meal was in the evening. This consisted of a cold starter, such as eggs or mushrooms, and then a main dish of roast meat or fish, followed by fruit.

Poor people bought what hot food they could afford from stalls in the town. All meals would have been washed down with grape juice, goat's milk, water or wine.

Banquets

A Roman banquet was an evening feast with many different courses. Among the special foods on offer were dormice in honey, flamingoes' or larks' tongues, and even elephants' trunks!

44

Clothes

The Romans liked to look good. Clothes showed off how important a person was, so rich Romans spent a lot of time on their appearance.

Roman women wore underclothes or a simple loincloth and perhaps a leather bra. Over this they wore a long *stola*, or robe. They then draped a large rectangular shawl, known as a *palla*, over one shoulder. Both *stolas* and *pallas* were usually made from brightly coloured cotton or, rarely, silk.

Men also wore loincloths. Their basic outfit was a simple woollen tunic made out of two rectangles stitched together and tied with a belt. This could then be covered with an elaborate toga.

A toga consisted of a long piece of woollen cloth wrapped round the body. It was so uncomfortable to wear that it was usually only worn on public or ceremonial occasions.

Roman Religion

The Romans worshipped many different gods. Farmers worshipped the nature gods that lived in the fields and woods. They made these gods happy with sacrifices and offerings at local shrines. Likewise, families offered presents to their household gods in return for their protection.

After their deaths, emperors were also thought to become gods. Showing respect to them was showing respect to the Empire itself. Each god had a dedicated temple and festival for worship and celebration.

The Pantheon in Rome was a temple dedicated to all the ancient Roman gods. It is one of the best-preserved of all Roman buildings and is now a Roman Catholic church.

Jupiter   Juno   Minerva   Cupid   Mars

The state religion of the Roman Empire was based on three main gods: the sky god Jupiter, his wife Juno, and their daughter Minerva, the goddess of wisdom. These three gods were joined by many others, with each different god or goddess looking after part of daily life. Cupid looked after love while Mars was responsible for war.

The coming of Christianity

Christianity arrived in Rome in the 50s CE and slowly spread throughout the Empire. However, Christians were often persecuted for their beliefs.

The Battle of Milvian Bridge

In 312 CE Emperor Constantine fought his rival Maxentius at Milvian Bridge outside Rome. He claimed he saw a cross in the sky with the command: *By this sign, conquer.* After his victory he said the sign came from Jesus Christ. This was a turning point for Christianity in Rome and more people began to follow the religion. Constantine stopped persecuting Christians and allowed them to worship openly. He paid for their churches and gave them important jobs. Constantine converted to Christianity on his deathbed.

Constantine believed that the protection of the Christian God helped his troops to a victory against the odds.

Pompeii

24 August 79 CE began as a hot summer's morning in Pompeii, a town to the south of Rome on the Bay of Naples. But during the day the sky got darker. Then, with a deafening bang, Mount Vesuvius suddenly erupted.

Mount Vesuvius was a dormant volcano, one that had been quiet for many years. When it erupted, it showered Pompeii and the neighbouring town of Herculaneum with tonnes of hot rock. A deadly cloud of gas and ash smothered people trying to escape. Just a few hours later, both towns were completely buried. Thousands of people lost their lives.

One witness wrote that the volcanic ash 'poured across the land' like a flood.

Rediscovery

The two towns remained buried for more than 1,700 years. Archaeologists began to slowly excavate the site in the 1700s. To their amazement they discovered the towns had been perfectly preserved. They found baths, a theatre, an amphitheatre and market stalls. They found streets full of shops and houses. Inside they found furniture and even food, such as eggs and bread. Because of all these finds, we now know a lot more about life in Roman times.

Preserving the dead

Archaeologists found the remains of more than 2,000 Pompeiians who had died in the volcanic eruption. Their bodies had been covered with ash that formed a solid case around them. Over the years, their bodies had collapsed, leaving their shape inside the solid ash. Restorers have now filled some of these shapes with plaster, so that we can see what the people looked like when they died.

Up in Arms

Not everyone liked being part of the Roman Empire. Throughout its history, many different people rose up in revolt against the Romans' rule. Two major revolts achieved notable success before they were crushed.

Boudicca

In 60 or 61 CE the Iceni tribe of eastern England revolted. The king of the Iceni had died and left his kingdom jointly to his daughters and to the Roman emperor. The Romans ignored his wishes and took the kingdom for themselves. The Iceni king's wife, Boudicca, fought against this. Her armies destroyed Colchester, London and St Albans, and defeated an entire Roman legion. Eventually, the Romans defeated the Iceni and their allies at the Battle of Watling Street, which was a Roman road between London and the Midlands. Boudicca killed herself and the rebellion ended.

Fierce Queen Boudicca was said to have long reddish-brown hair and wear a cloak fastened with a brooch.

The Jewish Revolt

A few years later, a much more serious rebellion broke out.
The Romans had ruled Jerusalem and the province of Judea
(in modern-day Israel) since 63 BCE. The Jews resented
Roman rule and rose up in revolt in 66 CE. A few years later,
the Romans regained control of Jerusalem after a siege in
70 CE in which they destroyed the main Jewish temple.

The hilltop fortress of Masada was attacked by the Romans in 73 CE and destroyed
in April 74 CE, finally ending the Jewish resistance.

Titus's arch

The Roman army that crushed the Jewish
revolt was led first by Vespasian and then
by his son, Titus. Titus became emperor of
Rome and when he died in 81 CE, a ceremonial
arch was built in Rome to celebrate his
victory over the Jews. The arch became the
model for many modern arches, including
the Arc de Triomphe in Paris, France.

Decline and Fall

The Roman Empire saw many changes after 200 CE. It was dealing with economic problems and frequent civil wars as its generals struggled for power. The western half of the Empire – including Gaul and Britain – temporarily broke away in 260 CE, while the eastern provinces briefly formed the independent empire of Palmyra. In 395 CE the Empire itself finally split in two (see page 23). A greater threat to Rome, however, came from outside its borders.

German invasions

The Germanic Goths, who lived to the north of the Black Sea, began to attack the Balkan provinces and Turkey from the 240s. Other Germanic tribes then flooded into the Empire over the German border. These raids grew more frequent in the next century. In 376 CE the Goths poured into Bulgaria and settled there. Two years later, the Romans tried to drive them out and were heavily defeated. War continued until Rome was sacked by the Goths in 410 CE. By now the Empire was under constant heavy attack from other German tribes and was falling apart. Roman troops also left Britain in 410 CE, as they needed to defend Gaul from invading barbarians.

As the Goths and others settled throughout the western Empire the German general Odovacer forced the emperor Romulus Augustus to resign in 476 CE. He was not replaced with another emperor. Rome had fallen and the Empire was at an end.

The eastern Empire

Unlike the western Roman Empire, the eastern part of the Empire (known as Byzantine) survived. In the mid 500s it reconquered Italy and North Africa and remained an important force in the Mediterranean until it finally collapsed in 1453.

The sack of Rome by the Goths was the first time Rome had fallen to an enemy in over 800 years.

What the Romans Did for Us

Although the Roman Empire fell apart over 1,500 years ago, its achievements live on. The Romans influence much of our modern life in many different ways.

Months and years

In 46 BCE Julius Caesar introduced the 365 and one-quarter day calendar. We still use this Julian calendar today. The names for all our months are taken from the Romans:

January	Janus, Roman god of doors
February	*februo*, the Roman word for 'purification'
March	Mars, Roman god of war
April	*aperire*, the Roman word for 'open'
May	Maia, the Roman goddess of growth
June	Juno, Roman queen of the gods
July	Julius Caesar, a Roman leader
August	Augustus, the first Roman emperor
September	*septem*, the Roman word for 'seven' (the Romans once started their year in March, so September was the seventh month of their year)
October	*octo*, the Roman word for 'eight'
November	*novem*, the Roman word for 'nine'
December	*decem*, the Roman word for 'ten'

Law and order

Roman law is still in force in much of western Europe, and the Roman use of a judge and a jury to hear court cases is common throughout the world.

Roman writing and numbers

This book is printed in a Roman type – that is, with upright letters. We still use the Roman system of numerals for numbers on some clocks and watches.

I	1	one
V	5	five
X	10	ten
L	50	fifty
C	100	one hundred
D	500	five hundred
M	1,000	one thousand

Latin

The ancient Romans spoke Latin, a language that is the basis for several modern European languages spoken today. There are many Latin words still used in the English language and Latin is officially used around the world for the scientific names of plants and animals.

dog
canis

Painted Lady butterfly
vanessa cardui

ivy
hedera

Religion

The Catholic Church was established during the days of the Roman Empire and is controlled by the Bishop of Rome, known as the Pope. Until the 1960s, the Catholic Church's services were all held in Latin.

Politics

Politically, the idea of the Roman Empire has lived on. In 800 CE the Frankish king Charlemagne was crowned Emperor of the Romans. In 962 CE, Otto of Germany became Holy Roman Emperor and his empire continued until 1806. Its symbol was the Roman eagle. More recently, the idea of a united Europe, as begun by the Romans, inspired the foundations of the European Union.

Famous Romans

Here are some of the greatest emperors and other notable people who helped shape or change the Roman Empire.

Augustus
(63 BCE–14 CE)
Called Octavian before he became the first Roman emperor in 27 BCE

Boudicca
(c.20–60/61 CE)
Leader of the Iceni revolt against the Romans in eastern England

Claudius
(10 BCE–54 CE)
The fourth Roman emperor, who invaded and conquered Britain in 43 CE

Cleopatra
(69–30 BCE)
Not a Roman, but the last pharaoh of ancient Egypt. Had affairs with both Julius Caesar and Mark Antony

Constantine I
(272–337 CE)
Emperor from 306–337. He created a new Christian capital of the Empire at Constantinople

Diocletian
(244–311 CE)
Ruled alongside another emperor. The Empire became so peaceful under him that he retired to a villa in Croatia

Hadrian
(76–138 CE)
Stopped the expansion of
the Empire and built walls and
defences to mark its borders

Hannibal
(247–182 BCE)
Led his army of Carthaginians
and elephants across the Alps
during the Second Punic War

Julius Caesar
(100–44 BCE)
Military leader, conqueror of
Gaul and dictator of Rome
until his assassination

Mark Antony
(83–30 BCE)
Rival for power in Rome with
Octavian. He was defeated by
Octavian at Actium

Nero
(37–68 CE)
An unpopular emperor who
was blamed for a fire that
destroyed Rome in 64 CE

Romulus and Remus
(c.700s BCE)
Legendary twins who were
rescued by a she-wolf. Romulus
became king and founded Rome

Tarquin the Proud
(535–496 BCE)
Lucius Tarquinius Superbus,
seventh and last Roman king
from 535 BCE until he was
overthrown in 509 BCE

Titus
(39–81 CE)
Military commander who
ended the Jewish revolt.
He was emperor from
79 CE until his death

Trajan
(53–117 CE)
Emperor from 98 CE, under
whom the Roman Empire
reached its greatest extent

Roman Timeline

800s BCE	Settlers arrive on two hills next to the River Tiber in Italy
753 BCE	The traditional date given for the founding of Rome by Romulus and Remus
717 BCE	Romulus dies
617 BCE	Roman power extends to the Mediterranean coastline
616–579 BCE	Tarquinius Priscus rules Rome and rebuilds it in stone
509 BCE	Tarquinius Superbus, the seventh king of Rome, is expelled and a Roman republic set up
494 BCE	Plebeians elect tribunes to represent their interests
396 BCE	Romans defeat neighbouring Etruscans after a long battle
390 BCE	Gauls sack and burn Rome
380 BCE	City walls built around Rome
367 BCE	Plebeians can become consuls
343–290 BCE	Romans defeat Samnites of central Italy in three wars
c.340 BCE	Romans defeat neighbouring Aequi and Volsci tribes
275 BCE	Romans defeat Greeks of southern Italy
264–241 BCE	First Punic War with Carthage; Rome gains Sicily, its first overseas colony
218–201 BCE	Second Punic War: Rome gains Spain
149–146 BCE	Third Punic War: Rome utterly destroys Carthage
146 BCE	Roman conquest of Greece
133 BCE	Pergamum in western Turkey becomes Rome's first Asian province
100 BCE	Birth of Julius Caesar
83–79 BCE	Civil war as generals fight for control of Rome
63 BCE	Romans first enter Jerusalem and rule Judea
58–51 BCE	Julius Caesar conquers Gaul
55, 54 BCE	Julius Caesar invades Britain
49 BCE	Julius Caesar crosses the Rubicon and enters Rome
48 BCE	Julius Caesar defeats Pompey in a civil war
46 BCE	Julius Caesar introduces a new calendar
44 BCE	Julius Caesar becomes dictator of Rome for life but is assassinated a month later by Brutus and Cassius
42 BCE	Octavian and Mark Antony defeat Brutus and Cassius in Greece
32 BCE	Octavian declares war on Mark Antony
31 BCE	Octavian defeats Mark Antony at the Battle of Actium
30 BCE	Mark Antony and Cleopatra take their own lives; Egypt becomes a Roman province

27 BCE–14 CE	Octavian is renamed Augustus and becomes the first Roman emperor
14–37 CE	Emperor Tiberius's rule
37–41 CE	Emperor Caligula's rule
41–54 CE	Emperor Claudius's rule
43 CE	Claudius invades Britain
50s CE	First Christians arrive in Rome
54–68 CE	Emperor Nero's rule
60 or 61 CE	The Iceni tribe, led by Boudicca, rise in revolt against the Romans in England
64 CE	A great fire destroys much of Rome
66–74 CE	Jewish Revolt against Roman rule
69 CE	Year of the Four Emperors
79 CE	Mount Vesuvius erupts and buries Pompeii
80 CE	Colosseum opens in Rome
98–117 CE	Emperor Trajan's rule
117 CE	The Empire reaches its greatest extent
117–138 CE	Emperor Hadrian's rule; he builds a long wall in Britain and defences in Germany
193 CE	Year of the Five Emperors
193–235 CE	The Severan family of emperors rule an increasingly crisis-ridden country
230s CE	Persians attack eastern provinces of the Empire
238 CE	Year of the Six Emperors
240s CE	Goths begin to attack Balkan provinces and Turkey
260 CE	Franks attack Gaul and Spain
260–274 CE	Breakaway Gallic Empire in western Europe and Palmyrene Empire in the east
285 CE	Diocletian rules alongside Maximian
307–337 CE	Emperor Constantine's rule
312 CE	Constantine wins Battle of the Milvian Bridge and stops persecuting Christians
313 CE	Christians become free to worship their god
330 CE	Constantinople becomes the new Christian capital of the Roman Empire
395 CE	The Roman Empire splits into western and eastern halves
410 CE	Visigoths sack and plunder Rome. Roman troops leave Britain
418 CE	Visigoths settle in western France
429–439 CE	Vandals conquer North Africa
476 CE	German general Odovacer forces last Roman emperor to resign

Dates before the birth of Christ are referred to as BCE, Before the Common Era.
Dates after Christ's birth are referred to as CE, in the Common Era.

Glossary

ally Country or person linked with another by treaty or friendship

amphitheatre Large, multi-seated open-air theatre where gladiators fought each other

aqueduct Pipe or channel carrying fresh water into a town or city

archaeology The study of the past using scientific analysis of remains

auxiliary Someone who provides a supporting role in the armed services

banquet A long, lavish meal consisting of many courses

besiege To surround a fortified town or military base with an army to try to conquer it

centurion Army commander of a century of eighty men

citizen A full member of a country with rights and duties

civil war A war inside a country between rival forces

consul The most senior government officer in republican Rome

convert To change from one religion to another

dictator A person who takes complete control of the state

dormant A volcano that has not erupted for many years

empire A group of different countries ruled by one nation

emperor	The ruler of an empire
engineer	A person who designs and builds machines or public works
fortification	A military construction, such as a wall or ditch, used to strengthen buildings or places
Gaul	The Roman province of France
gladiator	An armed fighter who fought for sport and entertainment in an amphitheatre
infantry	Soldiers who fight on foot
inherit	To receive money, property or a title from someone who has died
king	The male head of a royal family
latifundia	A large country estate
legion	The main fighting force of the Roman army, consisting of around 5,000 men
limites	The Roman word for borders or boundaries
marble	A hard rock used in buildings and statues that can be polished so that it shines brightly
merchant	Someone who buys and sells goods
moat	A ditch filled with water to keep an enemy out
paterfamilias	The Roman word for 'head of the family'
patrician	A rich Roman
persecute	To oppress or harm someone because of their beliefs
plebeian	A common person of Rome

Glossary

prisoner-of-war An enemy soldier captured during a battle

province An administrative district of the Roman Empire

republic A country without a king or queen, which is ruled by its people

resistance Fighting back against an enemy

reservoir A big lake or tank where water reserves are stored

sack To invade and destroy a town or city

sacrifice To kill an animal or person as an offering to a god

Senate The law-making parliament of Rome

shrine A place of worship to a god or group of gods

siege A military operation to capture a town or fort by surrounding and forcing it into surrender

slave A person owned by another to do menial work and who has no rights or freedom

strigil A knife-like instrument used to scrape off sweat and dirt in Roman baths

toga A ceremonial robe worn by Roman men

tribe A group of families or people with a common ancestor

tribunes Representatives of the plebeians

villa The large country residence of a rich person

Places to visit

Bignor Roman Villa, West Sussex

British Museum, London

Caerleon fortress, Monmouthshire

Chedworth Roman Villa, Gloucestershire

Fishbourne Palace, West Sussex

Hadrian's Wall, northern England

Housesteads Fort, Hadrian's Wall

Littlecote Park villa, Wiltshire

Museum of London, London

Porchester Castle, Hampshire

Roman Baths, Bath

Temple of Mithras, London

Vindolanda Fort and Museum, Hadrian's Wall

Index